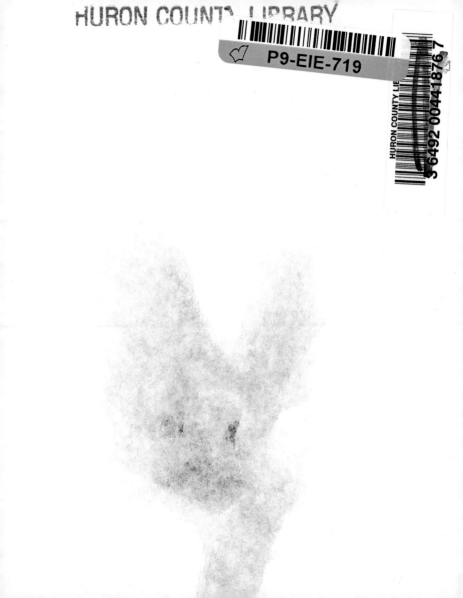

Baby Blessings

Baby Blessings

Inspiring Poems and Prayers for Every Stage of Babyhood

June Cotner

HARMONY BOOKS · NEW YORK

Published by Harmony Books, New York, New York.
Member of the Crown Publishing Group, a division of Random House, Inc.
www.randomhouse.com

HARMONY BOOKS is a registered trademark and the Harmony Books
colophon is a trademark of Random House, Inc.

Printed in the United States of America

Design by Jo Anne Metsch

Library of Congress Cataloging-in-Publication Data
Baby blessings : inspiring poems and prayers for every stage of babyhood /
[selected] by June Cotner.—1st ed.
Includes index.
1. Parents—Prayer-books and devotions—English. 2. Infants—Poetry.
3. English poetry. I. Cotner, June, 1950–
BL625.8 .B32 2002
242'.62—dc21   2001051528

ISBN 0-609-61017-1

10 9 8 7 6 5 4 3 2 1

First Edition

For my dear, sweet
Kyle and Kirsten,
who will always be my "babies"

Thanks

I AM VERY grateful for my children, Kyle and Kirsten. This book would not have been possible without their inspiration to me as their mother. My moments with them as babies are some of my most precious memories.

It is impossible to express how much I appreciate my husband, Jim. His love, encouragement, and patience are evident day after day. I am truly blessed to have a soul mate who gently keeps me anchored to my "real" life as a wife and mother.

I am eternally thankful for my agent, Denise Marcil, who has always guided me with wisdom and support. I owe much of my publishing success to her.

Linda Loewenthal, my editor at Random House, is a gem. She has made the passage from rough manuscript to this lovely collection a smoother journey, and the destination is far better than I had imagined, thanks to her talent and enthusiasm. I owe many heartfelt thanks to the wonderful staff at Random House: Cara Warner, Andrea Rosen, Liana Faughnan, Barbara Sturman, and Linnea Knollmueller. I am awed by their energy and their dedication to excellence.

There are so many people who worked behind the scenes to help me put together *Baby Blessings.* I feel a part of them is woven into the pages of this book. My space limits how much I'd really like to say, but I hope they know how very much I appreciate them: Gemma Arcangel (typing, filing, and so many errands), Cheryl Edmonson (book production and a myriad of tasks), Rebecca Pirtle (obtaining permissions, coordinating my publicity events, and an amazing amount of daily work), and Suzanne Droppert and her staff at Liberty Bay Books for all the help they are so willing to give me for the book's production and publicity. I owe another heartfelt thank-you to the staff at both the Poulsbo and Kingston Libraries who are so helpful in getting reference books for me.

The poems and prayers in *Baby Blessings* were subjected to several reviews, which included a test-market panel of eighteen critiquers. Thank you, critiquers, for providing me with invaluable feedback for the book! The panel included editorial staff from Harmony Books: Linda Loewenthal, Cara Warner, and Andrea Rosen; clergy: the Reverend Lynn James (a clinical counselor who copastors a church with her husband and contributed to *Family Celebrations* and two other books), Father Paul Keenan (author of *Heartstorming: The Way to a Purposeful Life* and two other books, cohost of the ABC radio program *Religion on the Line* and host of *As You Think*), and Rabbi Rami M. Shapiro (storyteller, poet, and author of *The Way of Solomon: Finding Joy and Contentment in the*

Wisdom of Ecclesiastes and five other books); poets: SuzAnne C. Cole (author of *Reading and Responding to Literature*), Barbara Crooker (prolific poet who has been published in six of my anthologies and winner of many poetry awards), Corrine De Winter (author of six collections of poetry and prose, including *Touching the Wound* and the poetry video collage *Recovery*), Maureen Tolman Flannery (editor of *Knowing Stones: Poems of Exotic Places* and author of *Remembered into Life*), and Donna Wahlert (Iowa/Florida poet who has been published in three of my anthologies); moms with new babies: Amelia Amos, Kelly Asadorian, Wendy Proffitt, Darci Thomas, and Deb Wensch; and my assistants (also moms): Cheryl Edmonson and Rebecca Pirtle.

I'd like to express a very special thanks to the wonderful poets and writers who contributed to this book; *Baby Blessings* represents their inspiring talent with words. I consider it a privilege to be able to work with you and share your work with the world.

My final thanks is to God, who has blessed my life with my dear husband and children; wonderful relatives, coworkers, and friends; work I love—and babies!

Contents

5. LULLABIES

9. INSPIRATION

Baby Blessings

A Letter to Readers

It has been a long time since I've had a baby of my own (my children are now in their twenties), and yet I can recall this time in my life with vivid clarity. I wouldn't trade the birthing pains, the sleepless nights, or the emotional roller coaster of being responsible for a tiny human life for anything else. Raising my children has been *the* most important and most difficult endeavor I have ever taken on. It has also been the most rewarding.

I wanted to capture the essence of this life-changing time in a book I could someday share with my children. I found it impossible to put into words all the emotions, hopes, and delight I had savored (and continue to cherish) from the moment I learned I held life in my womb. So, I began collecting poems that captured my feelings. As you can see, my collection has grown. In fact, it was very difficult for me to choose which ones would not be included in *Baby Blessings.*

In *Baby Blessings* you will find insight, joy, and inspiration for those wonderful years from pregnancy through every stage of babyhood. You will find many prayers and poems that can be used at baby-naming ceremonies, christenings, or for family gatherings. I included lullabies for those tender moments spent alone with baby. (Some mothers and fathers have told me they began singing lullabies to their children before they were born.)

I hope you enjoy this collection. I had fun putting it together. The poets represented here have a gift with words and many of their poems still bring tears to my eyes—even after reading them over and over. If you are a new parent, congratulations! Though at times exhausting and all-consuming, these early years with your child will always be remembered as some of your most treasured times. It's truly amazing how quickly they grow!

1

Pregnancy

Prayer for a New Family

Dear God,
Soon there will be three in this house
And we shall become a family.
Bless us each and every one
As we welcome this new soul
Who will change us forever.
Amen.

Betty Williamson

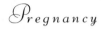
Pregnancy

I've heard all about
the dizziness of the mornings,
head hanging over the toilet rim,
fatigue as deep as the sea.

Still, I am eager for my body
to take over,
without the mind's righteous
interruptions.

I want to walk the streets with
my hands cradling my belly,
patting the burgeoning globe—
   my personal proof
that the world is round.

Andrea Potos

Leaving Their Mark

Stretch marks adorn my swelling body
like a lace gown, leaving indelible marks
that foretell my life, for to mother is to stretch:
stretch to make inborn nests,
to free these nestlings from my flesh,
stretch to feed them, help them walk, to
run and fly from my nest, where already
their lives are being written on my flesh
in stretch marks that are, really,
love lines on belly, soul, mind.

Margaret Anne Huffman
(1941–2000)

A Baby Is God's Opinion

A baby is God's opinion that life should go on.
Never will a time come when the most
marvelous recent invention is as
marvelous as a newborn baby.

Carl Sandburg
(1878–1967)

Freight Train

Swollen like a melon in July,
lumbersome as a moose,
I've boarded that train
and I can't get off,
no return trip.

Some babies are sweet
and pink as peaches;
others are wrinkled,
and scream like herons;
dispositions not optional,
all sales final.

Yet I know
that first cry
will bond me like glue,
and those wandering, wondering
dark eyes will fix my heart
faster than any lover.

Barbara Crooker

On My Daughter-in-Law's Pregnancy

Before you told us I knew—
knew by the way our son
draped his arm protectively
over your chair at dinner,
suddenly more mature than
when we last came together
and more joyous, laughing
at nothing, gazing often at
you and the secluded promise.

I knew by the way you
carried yourself, your step
both lighter and more careful,
knew by your choosing water
over wine, by the caress you
gave your belly when you
thought no one was looking.

But most of all I knew
by the light radiating from
both your faces, brighter
than the fireplace glowing
behind you, a mutual look
of tenderness and wonder.

SuzAnne C. Cole

Quickening

Some people call it butterfly wings
Or champagne bubbles
Or mermaids blowing kisses.
I call it "miracle."

Betty Williamson

Surprise

You were not expected.
Your presence caught us by surprise,
And we questioned, with some doubting,
This promised change upon our lives.
But the world has spun around, sweet child,
By a grace we cannot touch or see.
Somehow the dreams of two
Have grown to thoughts of "family"
While we await your coming
With all our hearts and every breath
Prepared for songs of welcome
And lullabies of tenderness.

Sharon Hudnell

The Answer of Love

We see it in
each other's eyes
every time our
daydreams touch,
that other part of us
that's soon to come,
that promise
that holds us
even when we sleep,
that little
answer of love
that soon will
fill the cradle
that now only rocks
in the corner
of our eyes.

Charles Ghigna

When You Slide Out Singing

I let my hand fall to rest
on the spot on my wife's belly
where her muscled flesh

has begun to rise, where inside,
unseen, the seed that is our child
has taken root, has taken hold

of my hand and set it down here,
where I rub the glowing skin
of this magic lantern and whisper:

child, oh child, when you slide out
singing into this new world light
we will be waiting, ready to dance.

Peter Markus

Delayed Motherhood Waltz

Lord, be with me—
I've come late to the dance,
Caught first by career,
Secure in the chance
For perfect timing.
Suddenly,
Time said: Decide.
Naïve, I expected
A smooth sweep and glide,
Not these spins of such joy
And these dips of some doubt—
It feels like my heart
Is inside out.
Please, Lord, take my hand,
And teach me the beat.
The steps I can learn
If you'll guide my feet.

Sharon Hudnell

You-and-I

Your spirit encircles me in ever closer rings,
lapping at my heart until I know
I am overtaken.
I plant a protective hand on my belly in a crowd.
Your father's lips hover over my waist wishing you good-night.

You sleep when I walk, awaken when I eat.
Your world of muted light and muffled sound, ruled by its
    own internal clock.
A baby dolphin, you kick out laps in your warm, salty sea.

Barefoot I dance upon the rug with you my silent partner.
Your father blows brilliant bubbles around us.
Iridescent orbs float from the wand and pop.

Soon, you-and-I will be
You
and
I.

Lynn Schmeidler

Waiting

Like birds await the morning,
　　Each one prepared to sing—
Like trees wait for the coming
　　Of their first new leaves of spring—
Like the shore waits for the evening tide,
　　Or the sun awaits the moon—
I wait to hold you, little one.
　　Child of my heart, come soon.

Sharon Hudnell

2

Birth

Parents' Prayer at the Birth of a Child

We are humbled by the awesome power of this moment.
From our lives we have brought forth life.
Through our love we have fashioned a child of love.

May our child be a blessing to all he meets.
And may he count us among his blessings as well.

Rabbi Rami M. Shapiro

Pre-Dawn Before His Birth

Sometimes when a sensation of warmth
comes over me
I think of that hour in the quiet house
before I would share him with the world,
salt water of his diving
having covered the land
like a tide at full moon and I,
lying there in the dark,
awake and waiting for another sign,
for movement, pain, the sky to crack open
and break the stillness.
No motion, only heat in the mountain of my middle,
deep, intense warmth as was there
in primordial timelessness before the thought
of earth had matured in the workings of God,
when only pockets of warmth floated about
in a space of divine nothing.
It was like that for the longest time
until he began his descent.

Maureen Tolman Flannery

Crowning

Like a shoot
pressing through
winter-packed earth,
the crest of head
emerges in the round mirror
set up near my birthing table.
I pant and push.
Here he comes—glistening,
like rain on a new bud.
His mouth opens.
At last, a cry.
Morning glory,
this son of mine.

Rochelle Natt

Star Child

I imagine you
budding purple
in my belly
like the tips
of new iris

My days shuffle
until the one
sharp with urgency
lays me down
to whelp

Come from song
at sunset
you are touched
with wine
plum dark

A thousand blooms
like secret shadows
drop sweet
through leaves of love

Tiny fingers
tremble golden
in the moonlight
June infant
star blessed

I shall celebrate
the night
whisper-wander
the universe
planet dance all summer

sing star child

Kate Robinson

My Wish for You

In my wish, you would be blessed
with friendships, happy and long.
Foundations would form in your life
to make you kind, caring and strong.

Curiosity would fill contented days,
creating respect, integrity and cheer.
The sun would rise with fresh adventures,
celebrating new chapters of your years.

In my wish, you would feel passion
for goodness, knowledge and trust.
Your life would be the model of one
that's upright, giving and just.

Into your heart, beliefs would be planted
that won't falter, fade or grow old.
You would reflect charity and trust
and blossom with the spirit in your soul.

Kathleen Haeny

Deliver Me

Our delivery room was in chambers.
A judge signed his name and our name was yours,
Not as messy as a hospital room,
But no nine-month warning: suddenly you
Were among us and one of us and we
Were with and for you. And we love you
For the same reason any parent loves a child—
Because God gave you to us, us to you.

Norman Styers

Our Son Was Born under a Full Moon

Our son was born under a full moon. That night I walked through the orchard, and the orchard was changed as I was. There were blossoms on the fruit trees, more white blossoms on the dogwood, and the tiny clenched fists of bracken shimmered silver. My shadow fell beside the shadow of the trees like a luster on the grass, and wherever I looked there was light.

Gary Young

At Last We Meet

At last we meet
Although I've known you forever.
First you were a dream,
Then a fuzzy blur of a sonogram,
And then soft stirrings
Of butterfly wings.
And then hiccups
And elbows and knees
Tickling my ribs.
And finally a slippery, beautiful
Lavender turning wiggly pink.
Happy birth day.

Betty Williamson

3

New Babies

Baby Fair

Baby fair,
Baby sweet;
Angel kisses
On your feet.

Tiny dancer
On the wing;
Your new voice
Is here to sing.

Baby love,
Baby mild;
Welcome, welcome,
Brand-new child.

Linda Robertson

Rejoice

(written in honor of the coming)

the clock has softly spoken
now now now with each
tick tock tick whispered

gather for the rejoicing

rejoice the cherubfat fists
curling fingers
tiny shell nails
eyes like a wet kitten freshborn
rejoice the marbling swirls of hair
rejoice the babybelly
rejoice the lungs grabbing air
for each sound proclaimed
rejoice the intricate lacing of
each eye closed with long long lashes
rejoice the arch of each foot
for its perfect kissing place
rejoice the peace that graces this house
    with dreamsleeps

rejoice the singing of
this new creation
this wondrous thing
this sacred gift

Kelly D. Matthews

New Baby

This place is radiant
with the simple, perfect grace
of you, beginning.

Tended by heartbeats,
you are the seed
of a tangle of dreams,
jewel-tones, opening
like wildflowers
in spontaneous brilliance,

visions of recipes
and heirlooms handed down.
Already we dance
at the celebrations
your life will bring,

where we will find ourselves
called together again and again
as this braid of lifelines
grows more and more entwined.

Kate Simpson

Simplicity

In the sheltered simplicity of the first days after a baby is born,
one sees again the magical closed circle, the miraculous sense of
two people existing only for each other.

Anne Morrow Lindbergh
(1906–2001)

The Beginning

You know that the beginning is the most important part of any work, especially in the case of a young and tender thing; for that is the time at which the character is being formed and the desired impression is more readily taken. . . .

Anything received into the mind at that age is likely to become indelible and unalterable . . . models of virtuous thoughts. . . .

Plato
(*c. 428—348 B.C.*)

Parents' Prayer at the Adoption of a Child

We are humbled by the awesome responsibility of this moment.
We are filled with joy and trembling
as we contemplate the tasks that lie before us:
modeling love, teaching courage,
instilling honesty, integrity, and responsibility.

May we come to embody the virtues we teach,
and may our child see in us
the values and behaviors we hope to see in him.

Rabbi Rami M. Shapiro

Colic

From the moment of birth
you cried in protest
as if the lights were too bright
sounds too stark
movements too sharp
air too chilled
as if rushed from the womb
without your approval.

Weeks later you still arch
your back, clench your fists
and cry until you're crimson
as if demanding to go back
to that muted world where
waves lapped to the rhythm
of intimate heartbeats.

But the two who waited
yearn to comfort and engage you.
Soon you will detect your mother's
smile as it rises in her eyes
and recognize the silk of her hair
as it catches in your searching fingers.

You will know your father's bearded
cheek as he presses his face to yours
and you will sleep easily
within the sling of his arm.

Donna Wahlert

My Preemie Son

I stand paralyzed
before the whole world
of your incubator,
stare at you
without blinking,
hoping my discomfort
will help you somehow,
take deep breaths
into my lungs, trying to
breathe for you, every
inhalation a prayer,
every exhalation,
heavenward.

Susan Rogers Norton

Infant

Fragile child, still
awkward in your small body
I hold you as if you
were made of glass,
frightened of moving the wrong way.
I am overwhelmed that you are mine,
that God has chosen me
to protect you.
I feel helpless at times
knowing
that one day you will
step into the world
and that I must know exactly when
to let you go.

Corrine De Winter

Prayer for a New Baby

We are grateful
for this new being
who is small in body
yet great in Soul,
who has come
into our midst
as a gift.
May we be sensitive
to the Sacred
as we nurture
and learn from
this child.
Give us patience.
Give us strength.
And grant us
wisdom and love
to help this child
learn to sing
his own song.

Anne Spring

Promises to a Newborn Daughter

Sleep now my little one, sleep curled
in comfort dreaming while I promise
to always see you as you are rather
than who I might wish you to be.

I promise to show you that
life is sacred, devotion worthwhile,
to teach you to value yourself
by honoring your autonomy.

I promise to share with you the rituals
of womanhood—trusting instinct and
intuition and respecting your body, its
mysteries and cycles of ancient rhythms.

I promise to show you the pleasure
of keeping a home and family—
and the pleasure of life outside the home—
friends, travel, sports and studies.

I promise that you will grow
in safety and comfort and that I will
share your tears, accept your defeats,
and rejoice in your triumphs.

SuzAnne C. Cole

Time Enough for Milestones

No firsts today, okay?
There is plenty of time for those
Tomorrow.
Today, just let me hold you
Watch you,
Absorb you,
Meet you.
And all those milestones?
They can wait.

Betty Williamson

All of You

I love all of you!
Your eyes, your cheeks,
Your sweet little nose;
Your knees, your feet,
Your stubby pink toes.

I love all of you!
Your dimples, your grin,
Your tummy, your chin,
Your ears, your hair,
Your lips, your skin.

Now, how did we get started?
How did we begin?
Oh, yes, I love all of you—
From beginning to end.

Annie Dougherty

Gift of a Grandchild

The clear plastic bassinet
reminded me of Cinderella's
glass slipper; both held magic.
She let me lift the baby,
put him in my arms, stroke
a cheek that had not yet
felt rain nor sun nor breezes.
My fingers kindled memory
of touching my own infants
and the privilege of life.
She's made me a grandma.

Lois Greene Stone

Remembered Rhyme

Long ago, when I'd forgotten how to rhyme
days, evenings, nights, and the dusky hours before dawn
were all consumed in milky sweetness

I nursed you on the sofa
at the kitchen table during dinner
out in the sunshine on the back porch
in the car, pulled over to the side of the road,
two wheels on asphalt, two on weeds

Rhyme was never completely forgotten, though
retained in soothing lullabies
Meter was kept in feet pacing the hall,
to hush your fussy crying
Rhythm maintained in the rocking chair,
creaking back and forth all those
late mornings
late afternoons
late nights
Really, I was never late for anything
because my clock was you

Toria Angelyn Clark

Head and Heart and Hands

Inside your head, your large, hard, floppy head,
Your brain is already folding around each new bit.
Into your brain, we will pack facts and fables and dates.

Inside your chest, every pulse a visible beat,
Your heart is pumping life from stem to stern.
Into your heart, we will pour love and care and balm.

Inside your hands, your fingers as fragile as wings,
Your palms' lines are foretelling ancient fortunes.
Into your hands, we will put pens and flowers, and thread.

Inside your head and heart and hands, we will place ourselves.

Martha K. Baker

Instinct

What good mothers and fathers instinctively feel like doing for
their babies is best after all.

Benjamin Spock
(1903—1998)

4

Babyhood

Prayer of Blessings

May you be blessed with a spirit of gentleness,
a heart that is tender.

May you be blessed with a spirit of strength,
shining within you.

May you be blessed with a spirit of compassion,
a fervent caring.

May you be blessed with a spirit of courage,
daring to be who you are.

May you be blessed with a spirit of openness,
understanding and respect.

May the earth hold you.
May the wind lift you ever up.
May the fire draw and warm you.
May the water quench and soothe your soul.
Amen

Deborah Cooper

Prayer to Baby's Angel

Dearest angel of my baby,
Guard his earth life well for me,
Lead him when I cannot be there.
See him where I do not see.

Follow him along the thorny
Places where he'll try to walk.
Help his words to please the starry
Heavens when he learns to talk.

Guiding spirit of my sweet child,
Protect him when I'm not around.
Boost his thoughts to rise unto you.
Keep his feet upon the ground.

Help me do my job as mother
While I sculpt his world view,
That, as he learns the stones and mountains,
He'll acknowledge your world too.

Maureen Tolman Flannery

Nursing

There is no sleep
like that which wraps you
closely in folds of well-being
with a baby at the breast
and all that's warm and safe
and full of possibility pressed
up against you like
the sunlight of a future summer.

Maureen Tolman Flannery

Two o' Clock in the Morning

It's two o'clock in the morning,
summer storm raging outside,
thunder cracking, dazzle of lightning,
branches dancing in the night wind.
But here in the nursery all is well.
The Mother Goose lamp glows,
the cushioned rocker gently glides.
Here's Mama, here's the breast,
Here's warmth and sustenance.

Satiated, you sigh, bubble of milk
balanced between perfect lips.
Your eyes open, focus on my face,
smile gratitude before sleep-heavy
lids gently close again.
Yes, all is well.
May it ever be so, Baby dear,
may we always be enough
to protect you from the storm.

SuzAnne C. Cole

I Could Call You Beautiful

I could call you beautiful
because you are mine.
I could say you will change the world
because I have a mother's faith in you.
I could say you will be loved by everyone
because I love you,
but today as I hold you in my arms
I can only say, dear baby,
I am so happy you were born.
Thank God!

Marion Schoeberlein

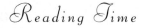

Reading Time

Reading time, our time,
just the two of us right now.
Lean your dandelion-drowsy head
against me just so, pop your thumb
into your mouth if you want, listen
while I read, as once long ago, your
grandmother read to me.

Mary, Mary, quite contrary . . .
Do you smell the heavy scent of lilacs
drifting through the screens?
A dillar a dollar . . .
Do you hear the fan clicking
its slow rotation?
Jack and Jill went up the hill . . .
Do you see the dust motes
flaring in the sunbeams?
Hickory dickory dock . . .
Hands on the grandfather clock
do-si-do a slow tick-tock.

Little one, this is life.

SuzAnne C. Cole

Momentary Grace

You reign in my lap, as
straight-backed as any czar,
surveying a backyard kingdom.
A butterfly, orange and black
dazzling in the sunlight,
alights on my leg. Shrieking
joyously, you lunge forward,
grabbing, but chubby fists
close on empty air.

I hold you close,
hug away your howls.
You do not understand how
holding too tightly destroys
a butterfly's fragile beauty,
or know as I do, that someday
I will have to let you too fly free,
but not, thank God, right now.

SuzAnne C. Cole

About the World

You talk
enamored of your sounds
gibberish, with an occasional word
that's comprehensible.

I catch you in these soft,
unnoticed moments
holding your stuffed dog up in the air,
telling him all there is to know
about the world.

Pamela L. Laskin

*E*cstasy

At eight months
you're positively pentecostal:
arms waving mid-air,
head tilted back—
swept off-balance by
life's new sensations.

Filled with spirit
you babble upward
to the sky or God,
engaging angels—
anyone—to speak your
tongue, to share your delight.

Then flesh overtakes you;
you slump exhausted
to the floor.
Your rhapsody spent.

Nancy Tupper Ling

Expectations

Insecure in my new role, I was at odds with—and battered by—an ideal of the breezy, capable mother I assumed everyone else was. I could handle myself at important meetings, meet tough deadlines, argue fluently in French. Why couldn't I keep Cheerios off the kitchen floor?

Leslie George

In That Moment, My Twins

yesterday they smiled at one another
my daughters'
toothless, gummy grins
that puckered their eyes and dimpled their cheeks
one on the right side and the other the left

and five months of simultaneous baby insistence
   piercing our nights
   offending our confidence
   swallowing our luxuries
   whole
   dining out, movie theaters, food shopping, phone calls,
     completing a sentence

washed over me
clean
as my twin baby girls
realized the friend
in one another

Kimberly Eagen Latko

First Steps

With the turn-out of a ballerina
she careens. Tiny quick steps
cross the floor. With percussion
of fleshy little soles set down,
first cautiously, wavering, then
with more and more abandon,
she perfects the upright art,
and raises hands,
in a gesture of awe,
or to encourage the applause
of her adoring fans.

Maureen Tolman Flannery

In the Deep Grace of Night

Wake in the deep grace of night
torn from some kind of dream
by blessed baby scream

Did you startle from a sudden thunder crash,
a car door slammed?
Or from hunger, from need
to suck my breast's milk cream?
I caress your sweaty head, hair swirling
rivers, your sticky fingers pinch my flesh

Maybe you woke just to hear me sigh
hush little baby don't say a word
and *all the pretty little horses*

lovely the sweetness of lullabies
sung softly in the dark, rocking

Toria Angelyn Clark

5

Lullabies

Song for an Unborn Child

Lullaby, little bird
sleeping in your nest,
Lullaby, little bird,
Mama loves you best.

Lullaby, little fish
Swimming deep and true,
Lullaby, little fish,
Mama's here with you.

Lullaby, little seed
Sowed in willing earth,
Lullaby, little seed,
Mama awaits your birth.

Little bird, little fish,
Little seed, little wish,
Little girl, little boy,
Little heart, little joy,

Lullaby, little soul,
Sleep until you're grown
Big enough, little soul,
To make the world your home.

Marjorie Rommel

Cradle Song

Sweet dreams, form a shade
O'er my lovely infant's head;
Sweet dreams of pleasant streams
By happy, silent, moony beams.

William Blake
(1757–1827)

Summer Lullaby

Moonlight,
Starlight,
Sweet potato pie

Mockingbird,
Hummingbird,
Flitting through the sky

Nap time,
Nighttime,
Summer lullaby

Betty Williamson

Lullaby

Slowly, slowly, slowly now
By the fading of the light
The day finds calm and comfort
In the silence of the night.

Softly, softly, softly now
Like whispers filled with love
The playful sounds of day are hushed
By the peace of stars above.

Sweetly, sweetly, sweetly now
Have dreams of rainbow hue
Oh, sleep well, my lovely one
God's blanket covers you.

Slowly, softly, sweetly now
God's blanket covers you.

Daniel Roselle

Slumbertime

Baby mine, close your eyes,
let me cradle
sleepy sighs

If I kiss that funny nose,
then, both knees
and bent elbows

I may giggle while you wiggle
all ten toes,
tiny toes

Baby mine, your gentle breath
is lullaby to me;
so, sleep, my love,
your father's here
holding all he treasures dear

Stephen Kopel

Brahms' Lullaby

Lullaby and good night,
With roses bedight,
With lilies o'erspread
Is my baby's sweet head.
Lay you down now and rest,
May your slumber be blessed.
Lay you down now and rest,
May thy slumber be blessed.

Johannes Brahms
(1833–1897)

All Through the Night

Sleep, my child, and peace attend thee,
All through the night;
Guardian angels God will send thee,
All through the night;
Soft the drowsy hours are creeping,
Hill and vale in slumber steeping,
I my loving vigil keeping,
All through the night.

Sir Harold Boulton

6

Baby-Naming Ceremonies

A Baby Naming Prayer

(L'Dor V'Dor*)

From generation to generation, we declare
God's praise. Today we rejoice
in celebration as we welcome you
into the covenant of Jewish family
to receive your Hebrew name.

Our heritage is a rich, colorful
cloth of many textures. We connect
the threads of generations
remembering our ancestors
whose lives made it possible
for you to be here today.

As we imagine your future,
we envision you weaving threads of Torah,
family and memory into a multi-faceted,
wondrous cloth which someday you
will hand down to your children.

*L'Dor V'Dor means "from generation to generation" in Hebrew.

As you grow, may the faith
that you cultivate
help you in both the difficult
and wonderful moments of your life.

May God direct you on the path of righteousness.
May your heart lead you to wise decisions.
May our family strengthen you.
May you discover the path most promising to you.
Amen

Sherri Waas Shunfenthal

Naming

We name you with love
We name you for courage
We name you with joy and for hopes not discouraged

We name you with pride
We name you for vision
We name you with laughter and for life's only mission

We name you with tenderness
We name you for love
We name you with blessings from heaven above

Jane King

Bless This Child

Bless this child, dear God, the One who brought him into our lives. Guide him on the path of goodness, mercy and loving kindness. Show him the blessings that arise when he remains connected with the Divine Source. And guide these parents to teach with love, compassion, patience and understanding, holding in their hearts a vision of what this child can grow to be, a person of his own choosing, but first and foremost, your Divine Creation.

The Reverend Edie Weinstein-Moser

A Prayer for Naming

May the Ineffable One fill this child with wonder
and joy.

May he seek only truth,
and make of his life a wellspring of healing.

May he come to discover his place in the world,
and have the courage to take it.

May he find wisdom in every blade of grass,
and knowledge in every clump of earth.

May he see the value of human striving
and the worth of human travail.

May he find health and happiness, wisdom and joy
in the world around and within him.

May he make room for the joy of discovery,
the pain of mistakes, the labors of freedom, and the risk of love.

May he who is called _____ grow in blessing
and attain the joy of wisdom, love, and good deeds.

May the life he will eventually lead
be a blessing to all who know him.

And let us say: Amen.

Rabbi Rami M. Shapiro

For a Naming Ceremony

Whose child is this?

This is the child of our community,
our hope for the future,
a child of earth, air, fire and water.

Whose child is this?

This is the child of love,
born of this woman and this man,
beloved of their families.

Whose child is this?

This is the child of God,
hidden in the bosom of the eternal
until this present moment.

Whose child is this?
This is the child of Life.

What name do you give this child?
We name him/her _____.

And we give thanks.

Maryanne Hannan

Identity

Little child,
next generation
of our family name,
may the strength of your roots
spark your ambition,
reflect your spirit,
and bring warmth
of family and fellowship
all the days of your life.

Kate Simpson

Naming the Name

We give you this first name.
May it flow like rivers of earth.

We give you this middle name.
May it warm from within like a heart.

We give you this last name.
May it stand for your heritage.
We give you our name.
May it honor your children, too.

Martha K. Baker

Here in . . .

Here in my heart,
Your name is Love.

Here in my voice,
Your name is Joy.

Here in my hands,
Your name is Hope.

Here in my mind,
Your name is Faith.

Here in my soul,
Your name is Life.

Here in this world,
Beloved child of God,
Your name is _____.

Sandra E. McBride

7

Christenings

A Christening Prayer

O God of all creation
You breathe life into every living thing
Your Spirit hovers near us
Protecting us, holding us, warming us
As a parent holds a child.

Come now and embrace this family
With your eternal love
And bless their child that she
May grow in grace and dignity
And find joy at every turn.

Sustain this family as they nurture their child
As they learn together, laugh together,
And share in the mystery of life together.
In unity may they excel in love and forgiveness
Valuing most highly the simple joy of being together.

Amen.

Kim Engelmann

Christening

Christen
this child
Dear Lord
with all your
grace and healing
your love and protection
Bring this child
into your
light,
forever and ever
Amen.

Paula Timpson

Baby Blessing

(Note: Insert baby's name on all lines.
For a baby boy, substitute appropriate pronouns.)

O Holy One, we gather here with joy on the occasion of
the christening of _____. Your gentle hands have
cradled this child to life and have gifted the earth with a unique
expression of your love. Give to those who will care for this
child strength, courage and wisdom as they begin this journey
of responsibility.

Bless _____ that she may grow strong in body
and spirit. May her lips speak the truth, may her heart find love
and may her feet always walk in the way of peace. May her
special gifts be recognized and developed that she may know
the joy of sharing them with others.

May your Spirit watch over and protect _____
both now and in the days to come. _____, may the
power and love of the Holy One bless you now and be with
you always.

Molly Srode

A Sense of Wonder

If I had influence with the good fairy
who is supposed to preside over
the christening of all children
I should ask that her gift to each child in the world
be a sense of wonder so
indestructible that it would last
throughout life,
as an unfailing antidote against
the boredom and disenchantments of later years,
the sterile preoccupation with
things that are artificial,
the alienation from the sources of our strength.

Rachel Carson
(1907–1964)

A Baptism Ceremony

Welcome

We are here today to give thanks to the Holy One as we cele-
brate a new life, the birth of _____ into the lives of
_____ and _____. You stand here today
and recognize that children are a gift of life, and that we who
are entrusted with their care are given both great responsibility
and great opportunity.

To parent a child is to affect the world, long after your lifetimes.
You will shape the future as you gently shape and influence
_____'s actions and thoughts. The sacrifices you
make to care for his needs, to stimulate his mind, to nurture his
heart, and to evoke his smiles, are investments that will bring
multiple blessings not just to your family, but to the world, in
ways you cannot even begin to know.

_____ and _____: Do you accept the
obligation which is yours, to love and to nurture, to teach and to

learn from this child who is in your care? Will you do all you can to keep his body safe from harm, fed, soothed, hugged, and strengthened? Do you strive to embody, for _____ and for each other, God's loving presence in your lives?

_____, I baptize you in the name of the Creator, Sustainer, and Redeemer. Amen.

_____ and _____, as _____'s godparents, do you promise to affirm and encourage, comfort and confront, support and sustain this child, celebrating with him in times of success and reaching out to him in times of sadness, surrounding him with your love and presence as he learns and grows?

Creator of all life, love, and beauty, we thank you for the love of family and friends so securely wrapped around _____ like a soft, warm baby blanket. We celebrate today a new life, a new love, emerging from the love shared between _____ and _____. Gracious God, give _____'s parents wisdom, humor, stamina, and the humility to ask for help when they need it. We appreciate the

tender touches of big sister/brother _____, and the
smiles that _____ gives back. We give thanks for the
grandparents so actively and joyfully helping to care for this
growing family. For all Your gifts into our lives, we give You
thanks and praise. Amen.

Candle Ceremony

At this time, the godparents, _____ and
_____, will light the candle on the altar. This is to
symbolize their promise to continue to give illumination to
_____ and to protect and encourage the light within
his soul.

Benediction

_____,

May your life be filled with laughter
May your heart be filled with song
May your eyes be filled with beauty
May your Soul always know to Whom you belong. Amen.

The Reverend Lynn James

Know You What It Is to Be a Child?

Know you what it is to be a child? . . .
It is to have a spirit yet streaming from the waters of baptism;
it is to believe in love, to believe in loveliness, to believe in belief.

Francis Thompson
(1859–1907)

aptism

Saturday afternoon, on a respite
   from cousins and aunts, we drift
      toward the sea, spellbound by a choir

of kites gathered in the sky. Unable to sneak
   space between worshipers and their airborne
      children, we salvage a quiet cove

up the road. There, free of priests,
   family and friends close
      in spirit, we three conceive

a private ceremony, slip off
   your white socks, kiss
      your diamond face, plunge

your crossed feet into an ocean
   calling your name. You
      savor the scent of salt, swirl

of your hair, depth
of the cold, catch a glimpse
of kite tails praising the sky.

Marybeth Rua-Larsen

Our Wish for You

May you always see beauty in the world
And hear music every day.
May you know the touch of gentle hands
And walk the peaceful way.

May the words you speak be loving,
May laughter see you through.
May you be blessed with hope and joy—
These gifts we wish for you.

Theresa Mary Grass

Blessing Wish-Song

May the blessings
   of the moon's changing cycles
and the blessings
   of the sun's constant providence
be with you
   as you enter your new world

May the blessings
   of this bountiful earth
and the blessings
   of rhythmic Mother Ocean
be with you
   as you walk your new path

May the blessings
   of family and friends
and the blessings
   of all in the web of life
be with you
   as you join us in a circle of love.

D. A. DeZormier

Waters of Life: A Christening

Today our small son* joins the ocean of life.
Let this water remind us of the waves he may encounter,
   or create.

Help us to prepare him for the ebb and flow of life's
   ever-changing seas.

Teach him to decide when it is wise to float with the current,
   or swim against the tide.

And lead him to that deep pool of faith, hope, and love within
   his own heart.

Sharon Hudnell

*For a baby girl, make the appropriate noun/pronoun changes.

8

Reflections

On Children

Your children are not your children.
They are the sons and daughters of Life's longing
   for itself.
They come through you but not from you,
And though they are with you yet they belong not
   to you.

You may give them your love but not your thoughts,
For they have their own thoughts.
You may house their bodies but not their souls,
For their souls dwell in the house of tomorrow,
   which you cannot visit, not even in your dreams.
You may strive to be like them, but seek not to make
   them like you.
For life goes not backward nor tarries with yesterday.
You are the bows from which your children as living
   arrows are sent forth.
The archer sees the mark upon the path of the
   infinite, and He bends you with His might that
   His arrows may go swift and far.

Let your bending in the archer's hand be for gladness;
For even as He loves the arrow that flies, so He loves
also the bow that is stable.

Kahlil Gibran
(1883–1931)

God's Message

Every child comes with the message that
God is not yet discouraged with man.

Rabindranath Tagore
$(1861-1941)$

Second Child Secrets

For the nine months you settled in, making yourself at home
   inside me,
tugging, flipping, kicking to make yourself known—
assuring you were getting my attention—
you seemed to already know there would be some competition,
that I had used up all my motherhood on your brother before
   you.
I was already spent from that deepest connection of purpose and
   awe.

As my body carried you, my heart carried the burden
of knowing that the second time, a second child—you—
couldn't equal the amazement I felt at each small
   accomplishment
when your brother developed and grew.
And knowing I couldn't again reach that height of motherhood,
fearing I would shortchange you, I vowed to spend every
   minute,
even as I held you in my womb, trying to make it up to you,
this lack of something already taken.

Baby Girl, you kept your secrets from me!
For in the instant I met you—my wondrous, spirited, enchanting
    daughter,
newly separate from me—you imparted a discovery
that began at your birth, the secrets you always held:
When I was carrying you, you were filling me
with the promise of you, and the extraordinary
baby child woman you would become.

Jane Butkin Roth

The Greatest Gift

If the Father in Heaven should say unto me,
　　"I will grant thee one wish, Mozelle.
So thou hadst best think deeply and long
　　So thou wilt wish wisely and well."

I'd not ask the Lord for a wonderful voice
　　Or for great fame untold.
I'd not ask for a beautiful face
　　Or for the glitter of gold.

I'd ask for something far greater than these,
　　The greatest gift from above.
Just a wee thing I could call all my own,
　　A dear little baby to love.

A dear little hand clasped tight in my own
　　A dear mouth made for me to kiss.
Of all the great things that the Lord could bestow
　　What gift could be greater than this.

Mozelle Schouten Leblanc

(1895–1951)

(Submitted by Jacque Hall, Ms. Leblanc's niece. She found this note in her aunt's dresser drawer after her death. Mozelle Schouten Leblanc never had a child.)

Song to a Lost Lamb

Tiny boy, three months premature,
delivered in rushing waves
yet born in silence:

you are an unblinking image
of your daddy—damp, soft curls
and fingertips
like petals from withered
pink rosebuds. As I cradle

your body in my hot, wet arms,
I, inhaling air for two,
must sing to you declaring
you are cherished

now and for all days
as much as any
warm and breathing child.

Susan Terris

To My Eurasian Grandchild

You herald a new dynasty
not with thunder, sword
or purple robe;
but with birth pang,
cord and bone
and the swaddling clothes
of brotherhood and peace.

You hold the promise of
a fifth season, an eighth sea.
You join the richness of Renaissance
and the stature of Ming.
You are a thought breathed by the Buddha
a prayer whispered by the Christ.
You are a new moment of grace in the cosmos.

Donna Wahlert

Caretakers of the Future

(After Immanuel Kant)

As we bring up our children, we have to remember that we are caretakers of the future. By improving their education, we improve the future of mankind, the future of this world.

Leo Tolstoy
(1828–1910)

Finding Balance

Ours is a society that places high value on achievement and acquisition. The subtle rewards of contemplation, quiet, and deep connection with another human being are held in low esteem, if they are recognized at all. As a result, mothers are constantly pulled in two directions: Can we negotiate the demands of our careers and the world at large, and meet our own emotional and physical needs—not to mention those of our children—at the same time? Can we keep our sights on what is important in any given moment? Do we know how to shut the door, stop the noise, and tune in to our own inner lives?

Katrina Kenison

Bond

The bond that exists
between mother and child
never dies. God is faithful
to remind us that love
and life are eternal and
that heaven is as close
as a whispered prayer.

Author unknown

Today

Today Noah is six
Blond, freckles, affectionate Junebug, cookie kisses & hugs
He will never again be 5, 4, 3, 2 or 1

Collector of feathers, rocks, sticks, seeds, nails, screws, yarn,
    broken pencils, business & birthday cards, coupons, maps,
    magazines, calendars, comics &
Paper, paper, paper
Today Noah is six

Lemon balm leaves, chamomile petals, peppermint pots: he
    owns gardens
Mason jars temporarily trapping beetles, moths & bugs
He will never again be 5, 4, 3, 2 or 1

Rescues empty shampoo bottles from the bathroom trash, fills
    them with water & arranges them on his windowsill
Loves peanut butter with apple butter sandwiches
Today Noah is six

Cuts, cuts, cuts paper into confetti
Epic sticky messes: Kool-Aid + margarine tub + forks + freezer
He will never again be 5, 4, 3, 2 or 1

Stolen herbal tea bags stashed in closet corners
What other hidden treasures and visions wait without condition?
Today Noah is six
He will never again be 5, 4, 3, 2 or 1

Toria Angelyn Clark

Normal Changes

At home with my new baby,
I suffered from sleep deprivation,
isolation, inability to concentrate
and the sense of days
spent treading wet cement.
Gray with fatigue, I asked a friend,
"Will it ever be normal again?"
"Normal changes," she replied.

Now, on the cusp of losing him,
first to college, then the world,
I am struggling with
sleepless nights, loss of appetite,
weeping spells, melancholia
and life's bittersweet lesson:
Normal changes.

Ann Reisfeld Boutté

You Give Up Your Self

You give up your self,
   and finally you don't even mind.
   I wouldn't have missed this for anything.
It humbled my ego and stretched my soul.
   It gave me whatever crumbs of wisdom
   I possess today.

Erica Jong

Mules of Love

for my daughter on her 21st birthday

When they laid you in the crook
of my arms like a bouquet and I looked
into your eyes, dark bits of evening sky,
I thought, *of course this is you,*
like a person who has never seen the sea
can recognize it instantly.

They'd pulled you from me like a cork
and all the love that had been bottled inside
flowed out. I adored you
with the squandering passion of spring
that shoots out green from every pore.

I was sure that kind of love would be
enough. I thought I was your mother.
How could I have known you were
the teacher sent to me. Over and over
you have cracked the sky like lightning,
illuminating all my fears, weaknesses, my sins.

Love this massive is the burden
we must learn to bear, like mules of love.

Ellen Bass

Our Fragile Emissary

With modern screening and such
they wonder why
you're here, on this earth,
in our home
and in our arms;
after all, anyone
with any sense
would have resolved
this problem of you
pre-birth, pre-pain.

Blonde Beauty,
tiny as you are,
you catch their stares,
strangers' second glances
into tender baby blues.
And your young
sweet ears hear whisperings
("Down's," "defects")
words dropped loosely
at extra-chromosomed girls.

With such stinging receptions
how we long to shelter you,
surround you; keep your
gentle smiles to ourselves.
Instead, we hold you
up, for others to see;
let you, our fragile emissary,
speak to an imperfect world.

Nancy Tupper Ling

The Courage to Love

Love is the most democratic act imaginable. It is the great equalizer. Not everyone has the opportunity, luck, or skill to become a great filmmaker, architect, businessman, artist, or professor. But anyone with the courage to love can earn the privilege of sitting on a park bench and having someone—a child, a granddaughter, an adopted son—stroke their hand and say, "You're the greatest thing that has ever happened to me." That is the ultimate test of greatness, the ultimate test of freedom, the ultimate rebellious act. That kind of love, family love, makes us powerful beyond measure.

James McBride

9

Inspiration

A Mother's Prayer

Of all the tasks I will undertake in my lifetime, there is none
more important to me than being a good mother. Please guide
me every step of the way. Remind me that my every word and
deed is being watched by my children. My life must be a pattern
for them to follow. No matter what I achieve in my life it will
not matter if I fail as a mother. Please help me get it right.

Amen

Teresa B. Kindred

We Are Their First Teachers

True happiness is found within ourselves and in quiet harmony with others. Yet if we let this inner knowledge slip away, our children may never learn it themselves, for we are their first teachers. It is up to each of us to set the example, to show by our own actions our respect for intimacy, contemplation, and wonder. This is perhaps the greatest legacy we can bestow on our children: the capacity to be enchanted by the quiet gifts of everyday life.

Katrina Kenison

Living by Example

Your life is your message to your children.

Gandhi
(1869–1948)

My Son

You did not come to me as the moon, reflective
of me, or to orbit my life but as a star, radiant
with light and warmth and path of your own.
I will try always to remember.
I want neither to hold you captive to my dreams
nor to pressure you to color between lines I have drawn.
I hope never to distort your questions
to fit my answers; but sometimes
I will forget.
May the limits I set serve you
like the scaffold serves the skyscraper in its ascent,
then falls away when the time comes to let go.
May my words teach you to listen
and my listening teach you to speak
so in quiet it is your own voice you find.
May I be a mirror so you see yourself clearly
as child of a loving God who delights in your being.

Barbara Shooltz Kendzierski

Soft Moccasins

May your baby wear soft moccasins.
Let him know the bending of grass
the hardness of stone.
Let him feel the leaves there, then gone
and find the seasons walk with him.

May his steps take him
from the arms of family to the eyes of friends.
Let him learn the difference between
those who feel his presence
and those who listen for his coming.

May his steps bring him
through the glare of clearings
and shadows of thickets
until he kneels at the river
and drinks from his own hands.

Let your son pause to see there
dancing in the currents
a face much like your own
a face soft yet strong enough
to carry him home.

Linda Elena Opyr

Mother's Prayer

Teach me to walk slowly
    with my children, Lord,
To talk quietly and with
    assurance.
Let me give them hope not fear.

Help me to listen to their
    voices, Lord,
So I may know when the sound
    is idle chatter,
And when it is the cry
    of a lonely heart.

Teach me to share my joys
    and restrain my disappointments.
Precious Lord, light my way,
    let me be a good example
Of a loving spirit.

Marilyn Giese

A Parents' Prayer

We call unto the Source of Life
in thanksgiving for the wonder of this gift of life.
We are humbled by the blessings
and responsibilities of parenthood
and our participation in the miracle of creation.

May we learn to love without smothering.
May we learn to house without imprisoning.
May we learn to give without imposing.
May we learn to live today,
that yesterday and tomorrow
might find their own way in the world.

We give thanks to Life for the gift of life,
and stand in wonder
before the awesome task of parenting that lies before us.
Blessed is the Way of Life
that makes parent rejoice with child.

Rabbi Rami M. Shapiro

Author Index

Permissions

GRATEFUL ACKNOWLEDGMENT is made to the authors and publishers for the use of the following material. Every effort has been made to contact original sources. If notified, the publishers will be pleased to rectify an omission in future editions.

Alfred A. Knopf for "On Children" from *The Prophet* by Kahlil Gibran. Copyright © 1923 by Kahlil Gibran and renewed © 1951 by Administrators C.T.A. of Kahlil Gibran Estate and Mary G. Gibran. Reprinted by permission of Alfred A. Knopf, a division of Random House, Inc.

Martha K. Baker for "Head and Heart and Hands" and "Naming the Name."

Ellen Bass for "Mules of Love."

Ann Reisfeld Boutté for "Normal Changes."

Toria Angelyn Clark for "In the Deep Grace of Night," "Remembered Rhyme," and "Today."

SuzAnne C. Cole for "Momentary Grace," "On My Daughter-in-Law's Pregnancy," "Promises to a Newborn Daughter," "Reading Time," and "Two o'Clock in the Morning,"

Susan Rogers Norton for "My Preemie Son."

Linda Elena Opyr for "Soft Moccasins."

Peter Pauper Press Inc. for "A Mother's Prayer" from *A Mother's Prayer* by Teresa B. Kindred. Copyright © 1995 by Peter Pauper Press. Reprinted by permission of Peter Pauper Press.

Andrea Potos for "Pregnancy."

Linda Robertson for "Baby Fair."

Kate Robinson for "Star Child."

Marjorie Rommel for "Song for an Unborn Child."

Daniel Roselle for "Lullaby."

Jane Butkin Roth for "Second Child Secrets."

Marybeth Rua-Larsen for "Baptism."

Lynn Schmeidler for "You-and-I."

Marion Schoeberlein for "I Could Call You Beautiful."

Rabbi Rami M. Shapiro for "A Parents' Prayer," "Parents' Prayer at the Adoption of a Child," "Parents' Prayer at the Birth of a Child," and "A Prayer for Naming."

Sherri Waas Shunfenthal for "A Baby Naming Prayer."

Kate Simpson for "Identity" and "New Baby."

Anne Spring for "Prayer for a New Baby."

Molly Srode for "Baby Blessing."

Lois Greene Stone for "Gift of a Grandchild."

Norman Styers for "Deliver Me."

Susan Terris for "Song to a Lost Lamb."

Paula Timpson for "Christening."

Donna Wahlert for "Colic" and "To My Eurasian Grandchild."

Rev. Edie Weinstein-Moser for "Bless This Child."

Betty Williamson for "At Last We Meet," "Prayer for a New Family,"
   "Quickening," "Summer Lullaby," and "Time Enough for Milestones."

Gary Young for "Our Son Was Born Under a Full Moon."

Permissions compiled by Rebecca Pirtle.

Photo Credits

Grateful acknowledgment is given to the following individuals for the photographs that appear in this book.

First half title page: Amelia Anne Parker, © Anne Darby Parker; "Pregnancy": June Cotner Graves and son Kyle Myrvang, from the author's private collection; "Birth": Taylor Alexander Hartmann, © Jill A. Hartmann; "New Babies": Amelia Anne Parker, © Anne Darby Parker; "Babyhood": Peggy Tillery, photographer unknown; "Lullabies": Katrina Kenison Lewers and Jack Lewers, © Anne Darby Parker; "Baby-Naming Ceremonies": Amelia Anne Parker, © Anne Darby Parker; "Christenings": Georgia Darby and Litsa Darby, © Anne Darby Parker; "Reflections": Sana Weiher Keller, © G. E. Weiher; page 151: subject unknown, © Anne Darby Parker.

About the Author

JUNE COTNER is a bestselling author, anthologist, and speaker. Her books include *Mothers and Daughters* (published by Crown Publishers); *Graces, Bedside Prayers, Get Well Wishes*, and *Animal Blessings* (all published by HarperCollins San Francisco); *Amazing Graces* and *Teen Sunshine Reflections* (both published by HarperCollins Children's Books); *Family Celebrations* and *Heal Your Soul, Heal the World* (both published by Andrews McMeel); and *The Home Design Handbook* (Henry Holt and Company). All together, her books have now sold more than 500,000 copies. She has four forthcoming anthologies. June's books have been featured in many national publications, including *USA Today, Better Homes and Gardens, Woman's Day*, and *Family Circle*, as well as on national radio programs.

June has taught workshops for writers and given presentations at bookstores throughout the country and at the Pacific Northwest Writers Association Conference, at the Pacific Northwest Booksellers Association Conference, and at The Learning Annex in New York, San Francisco, Los Angeles, and San Diego. For information on scheduling her as a speaker or workshop leader, you may contact June at one of the following addresses.

A graduate of the University of California at Berkeley, June has an impressive background of twenty-five years in marketing. She is the mother of two grown children and lives in Poulsbo, Washington (a small town outside of Seattle), with her husband, two dogs, and two cats. Her hobbies include yoga, hiking, backpacking, cross-country skiing, and gardening.

June Cotner
P.O. Box 2765
Poulsbo, WA 98370
june@junecotner.com
www.junecotner.com